KT-513-268

HOPSCOTCH
TWISTY TALES

The Beautician
and the Beast

by Karyn Gorman and Kelly Kennedy

C334045545

This story is based on the traditional fairy tale,
Beauty and the Beast, but with a new twist.
Can you make up your own twist for the story?

For Holly – K.G.

Franklin Watts
First published in Great Britain in 2016 by The Watts Publishing Group

Text © Karyn Gorman 2016
Illustrations © Kelly Kennedy 2016

The rights of Karyn Gorman to be identified as the author
and Kelly Kennedy as the illustrator of this Work have been asserted
in accordance with the Copyright, Designs and Patents Act, 1988.

All rights reserved.

ISBN 978 1 4451 4797 0 (hbk)
ISBN 978 1 4451 4799 4 (pbk)
ISBN 978 1 4451 4798 7 (library ebook)

Series Editor: Melanie Palmer
Series Advisor: Catherine Glavina
Series Designer: Peter Scoulding
Cover Designer: Cathryn Gilbert

Printed in China

Franklin Watts
An imprint of
Hachette Children's Group
Part of The Watts Publishing Group
Carmelite House
50 Victoria Embankment
London EC4Y 0DZ

An Hachette UK Company
www.hachette.co.uk

www.franklinwatts.co.uk

MIX
Paper from
responsible sources
FSC® C104740

FSC
www.fsc.org

Once upon a time there lived a
beautician named Belle, who was
not only beautiful but very skilled.

She was the kingdom's best hairdresser and everyone went to her for the latest looks.

"There you are. I think you'll find this stylish bob much more practical," said Belle.

"Thanks," chirped Rapunzel.

"I overslept!" cried Sleeping Beauty. "Can you still fit me in?"

"Yes, straight after I finish Cinderella's hair. She's got an important ball tonight," sang Belle.

Belle would twirl and swirl and snip happiness wherever she went.

But there was one place in the land that her beauty could not reach.

9

High on the tallest mountain lived
a most ferocious beast. His body
was bushy, his mane was messy,
and no matter what anyone said,
he refused to cut his hair.

"It's just not my style,"
claimed the Beast.

Then, one day, the Beast's hair became so overgrown that it blocked out the sun. Darkness fell upon the kingdom. No one could see anything.

"Mirror, Mirror, on the wall ... where are you?" cried the Queen.

Something had to be done.
By royal decree every barber,
stylist and beautician in the land
went to the castle to try to
convince the Beast to cut his hair.

"How about curls?" said one.
"No, clean cut is best," claimed
another.

But the Beast refused them all.
Eventually everyone gave up,
yelling that the task was
"impossible", "ridiculous", and
even a bit dangerous.

Only Belle remained.
"Would you mind if I stayed
a while?" she asked.

Belle knew that beauty could be revealed in unexpected ways. So she decided that the best way to find the right look for the Beast was to get to know him.

Belle and the Beast walked
and talked.

Belle did the Beast's chores around
his castle.

Belle told the Beast about her dream to spread beauty to the whole land.

"You already do," the Beast told her.

Then one night, after much convincing, Belle got the Beast to sit in her chair.

When the sun rose the next morning, the whole kingdom rejoiced and waited…

But when Belle and the Beast arrived, the town was shocked.

Belle had not cut one hair on the Beast's head.

"Sometimes, beauty is revealed in unexpected ways," said Belle as the Beast showed off his new mane.

Everyone agreed that the Beast
was indeed very stylish and the
kingdom lived happily ever after –
at least they did after getting the
same hairdo.

Puzzle 1

Put these pictures in the correct order.
Which event do you think is most important?
Now try writing the story in your own words!

Choose the correct speech bubbles for each character. Can you think of any others? Turn over to find the answers.

Answers

Puzzle 1

The correct order is: 1c, 2b, 3e, 4a, 5d, 6f

Puzzle 2

Belle: 1, 3, 4

The Beast: 2, 5, 6

Look out for more Hopscotch Twisty Tales

The Ninjabread Man
ISBN 978 1 4451 3964 7
The Boy Who Cried Sheep!
ISBN 978 1 4451 4292 0
Thumbelina Thinks Big
ISBN 978 1 4451 4295 1
Move versus the
Enormous Turnip
ISBN 978 1 4451 4300 2
Big Pancacke to the Rescue
ISBN 978 1 4451 4303 3
Little Red Hen's Great Escape
ISBN 978 1 4451 4305 7
The Lovely Duckling
ISBN 978 1 4451 1633 4
Hansel and Gretel
and the Green Witch
ISBN 978 1 4451 1634 1
The Emperor's New Kit
ISBN 978 1 4451 1635 8

Rapunzel and the
Prince of Pop
ISBN 978 1 4451 1636 5
Dick Whittington
Gets on his Bike
ISBN 978 1 4451 1637 2
The Pied Piper and
the Wrong Song
ISBN 978 1 4451 1638 9
The Princess and the
Frozen Peas
ISBN 978 1 4451 0675 5
Snow White Sees the Light
ISBN 978 1 4451 0676 2
The Elves and the
Trendy Shoes
ISBN 978 1 4451 0678 6
The Three Frilly Goats Fluff
ISBN 978 1 4451 0677 9

Princess Frog
ISBN 978 1 4451 0679 3
Rumpled Stilton Skin
ISBN 978 1 4451 0680 9
Jack and the Bean Pie
ISBN 978 1 4451 0182 8
Brownilocks and the Three
Bowls of Cornflakes
ISBN 978 1 4451 0183 5
Cinderella's Big Foot
ISBN 978 1 4451 0184 2
Little Bad Riding Hood
ISBN 978 1 4451 0185 9
Sleeping Beauty –
100 Years Later
ISBN 978 1 4451 0186 6
The Three Little Pigs &
the New Neighbour
ISBN 978 1 4451 0181 1

For more Hopscotch books go to:
www.franklinwatts.co.uk